Side by Side

I0154984

By Diane Silcox Jarrett

Illustrations by Carol Moates

Jingle Books
Indigo Sea Press
PO Box 26701
Winston-Salem, NC 27114

This book is a work of creative non-fiction.

Copyright 2017, Diane Silcox Jarrett

All rights reserved, including the right of reproduction in whole or part in any format.

First Jingle edition published
January, 2017
Jingle Books, Moon Sailor, and all production design are trademarks of Indigo Sea Press, used under license.

For information regarding bulk purchases of this book, digital purchase and special discounts, please contact the publisher at indigoseapress.com

Diane Silcox Jarrett, Author
Carol Moates, Illustrator

Manufactured in the United States America
ISBN 978-1-63066-249-3

Dedication:

To Alex, who enjoys jazz with me.

To Ken and Mike, who are always ready for a jazz concert.

Thank you Shari for the title idea.

Have you ever felt a beat from your heart to your toes? It catches you by surprise you want to jump out of your seat. Your feet can't stop tapping. You hum right along. Before you know you're a part of the music. It's swing, it's bebop, it's jazz.

Two musicians, Thelonious Monk and John Coltrane felt that rhythm and beat from their hearts to their toes. That beat filled them up so much it spilled out into their music.

Both were born in small North Carolina towns, Thelonious only nine years before John. The two boys grew up in Southern summer nights, the moon gleaming overhead and the creepy-crawlers squirming out. They caught fireflies while mosquitoes bit their legs. The buzz of insects and croaking of frogs blended together. Night critter harmony got louder and louder as the night grew darker. Each creature's melody blending into a summer synchronized song.

Thelonious was just four (and John wasn't born yet) when he said goodbye to those fireflies and night critters sounds. There was a big world beyond his small town of Rocky Mount, and his mother wanted her children to experience it. Thelonious, his older sister and younger brother moved to New York City, where buildings towered so far above him Thelonious had a hard time seeing the sky. New noises caught Thelonious' ear just as the night critters had before. Music from all over the world flowed from open windows on warm summer nights. Melodies and tunes from Jamaica, Cuba, and Mexico mixed with the chatter from the streets, and the bustle of cars and buses.

It wasn't long before Thelonious' family had music flowing from their apartment when his mother bought a piano. The keys moved like magic as though there was an invisible person making them skip up and down. Thelonious stared at those keys closely as his sister practiced. When he started playing it was if his fingers had been waiting for the piano, and the piano had been waiting for him. Music morning, noon, and night, his fingers didn't want to stay away. On summer nights his mother took her children to Central Park to hear the sounds of an orchestra and the blend of instruments weaved through the crowd right into the children's ears.

As Thelonious grew, his love for the piano did too. He practiced and practiced. He played hymns on an organ at church, people loved to hear him at parties, and he became part of a trio that took jobs wherever they could find work. Monday nights at Harlem's Apollo Theater were known as "Audition Night." If the audience voted you the best ten dollars was yours. The trio won so often, they were asked not to come back.

Thelonious needed steady work so when the chance came to travel with a female evangelist, he left New York. The familiar hymns he'd learned from his mother kept him from being too homesick. But after two years he was ready to go home. He missed his family; he missed the city, he missed the energy it gave him.

Minton's Playhouse in Harlem became his new musical home. When the lights came up, he joined other great young jazz musicians on stage. They had their own ideas, their own way of playing. On Monday nights, they had crazy jam sessions filled with laughter, chatter, and challenge. Could you hold your notes longer? Could you change up the melody and chords? Each musician had his own way of feeling and expressing the music. They played spontaneously and individually but when they put them together, the music worked. It had new rhythms, and a surprising new style. It had a name: bebop. "If you really understand the meaning of bebop, you understand the meaning of freedom." Thelonious said.

Thelonious played with many groups, keeping his ears open to learn. He had his own technique—a string of rapid notes and then a pause, it was all Thelonious. He composed his first big song, "Round Midnight," a melancholy tune that sounded sad and happy at the same time. Before long, he noticed other musicians playing his music. Thelonious worked on his songs until he felt they were perfect. He said, "When the song tells a story, when it gets a certain sound, then it's through….completed."

While Thelonious was making music in New York, John Coltrane was growing up in High Point, North Carolina. He lived in his grandfather's house with parents, his cousin Mary and her family. John went to segregated schools where he learned from second-hand school books the white schools had discarded. John didn't like the torn, scrawled-on pages. But he studied anyway. Listening to the radio helped, and brought his favorite music right to him. Popular swing tunes like, "One O' Clock Jump", and "Take the A Train" set John toe-tapping as he worked his way through long division problems.

He loved the sound of the smooth sax soaring through the notes like a hawk gliding through the fall skies. Listening to the music helped make the ways of the world go away. There was other music in the house too. John grew up with a player piano like Thelonious and his father played the ukulele. His mother's singing voice could be heard from room to room as she went about her day.

When he was twelve, the two men John loved the most died—his father and grandfather. Sadness overcame John, and his mother. John knew music would make him feel better. He decided to join the Community Band. He played the alto horn and the clarinet. From the first note he blew, it felt calming and all the sadness ran from his heart into his horn.

It was tough for John's mother to make ends meet. To help out John shined shoes at a country club, but it wasn't enough. His mother had to rent out some of the family's rooms. John, his cousin Mary, and his aunt slept in the dining room. Not having a private place to be alone with his music was much worse for John than losing his bed. When his high school started a band John joined up and played the alto sax. During his high school years, John's mother decided it was time for a change and moved to Philadelphia. Like Thelonious' mother, she was hoping to find a better life. John stayed behind to finish high school. He lived at home with renters and played in the high school band eager to get home to practice every day. If he had music everything seemed all right.

After graduation, John was ready for Philadelphia, and Philadelphia was ready for him. The city had so much to offer. On the busy streets people called out to each other, buses sloshed water up on the curbs, car horns honked in a constant beat. Philadelphia was full of so much liveliness and full of jazz. Cold winter rain seeped through John's shoes as he walked to the library where he listened to tapes of classical music over and over, concentrating on each note.

Still, time alone was his favorite. John faced a wall in the apartment to remove distractions as his fingers moved swiftly on the used tenor saxophone his mother bought him. He wanted to master every note. The neighbors complained, but if they had only listened closer, they would have heard John's sweet tones.

"I find it's only when something is trying to come through I really practice. And then, I don't know how many hours. It's all day," said John.

After hours and days of practice, John became a part of the musical world around him adding his saxophone style at clubs and dances. He listened and played with other musicians but he knew in his heart he had to have his own individual style and technique. He wanted his music to be precise. Though he loved jamming, practices and performing, they consumed the exhausted John and he became overwhelmed. Even with his dreams coming true, the late hours and full days ran into each other. Other musicians thought his playing wasn't as good as it should be. He lost some jobs. This was hurtful and hard, but John knew he was the only one who could help himself.

Once again, as he had when he was younger, John turned to his saxophone for comfort. Its soulful wails helped him heal and within a year John recorded his first album, "Coltrane," which included a song he composed, "Chronic Blues" – upbeat notes flowing like a silky journey. John still wanted to learn more. So he moved to New York where its vibrant jazz led him to new discoveries.

New York City sizzled in the summer of 1957. Children jumped in the spray of fire hydrants to cool off. Fans didn't help; they only blew the hot air around. By noon your shirt stuck to your skin and left you longing for a cold drink.

It wasn't long before John met Thelonious and they played together several times. John sensed Thelonious had much to teach him. Walking to Thelonious' apartment John anticipated the time ahead, and imagined the questions he would ask. How long should he hold a note? Would certain notes make the music sound better? Some questions could only be answered through the piano and Thelonious' fingers acted as the teachers as they touched the keys. John listening carefully, determining which note he'd hit where he'd pause and when he'd speed up or slow down.

Again and again, John repeated bits that seemed difficult until he grasped them. After a while Thelonious left the apartment. He wanted John to feel the music by himself, not just memorize it. John held the saxophone until his hands ached, blowing into it for hours, notes swirling around him in the warm muggy air.

When Thelonious returned, he listened patiently to John's chords and harmonies, coaching him on little things that needed attention. Side by side, the men perfected their sound.

"I learned a lot with him," John said of Thelonious, "I learned little things, you know, I learned to watch little things…Little things mean so much in music, like in everything else."

That summer John joined The Thelonious Monk Quartet. The quartet filled people's ears and word got out. Before long, fans were lining up for jazz tempos, rhythms and beat that made them forget the heat and return night after night.

With the lights beaming down on the stage and the heavy hot air, Thelonious sweated so much his wife made handkerchiefs out of sheets so he could wipe his brow. He became known for wearing his sunglasses and a variety of odd hats - bobble hats, berets, pork-pie hats, and skullcaps. The piano keys sent music like electricity from his fingers right down to his toes till he bopped across the stage with a shuffle and a spin, pumping his elbows, his body keeping up with the band's perfect beat.

Intense and free flowing was the way John played. You could hear the details of each note clear and concise. John's focus was so intent, it was though he became a part of each piece he played.

The Thelonious Monk Quartet performed right into the fall. Lines of fans grew longer as their music became more popular. When the Thelonious Monk Quartet was invited to perform at Carnegie Hall to raise money for a community center, Thelonious and John remembered their childhood struggles and wanted to help. They joined other musical stars to put on a show that lit up the fall New York City night.

It was the evening after Thanksgiving, and inside the famous hall wood floors sparkled with polish, and the lights reflecting the wonder of the night. As John wrapped his fingers around the cool metal of his saxophone from across the room, he caught a quick smile from Thelonious.

In one of most famous concert halls in the world, two men, full of spirit and energy captured the audience as they'd once caught fireflies in the North Carolina moonlight. Thelonious' fingers cascaded over the piano's keys, filled with liveliness and as mellow as the moon. John's saxophone echoed off the hall's walls, smooth and rich. Side by side they stirred the audience with their dreamy rendition of "Monk's Mood" and the vibrant notes of "Nutty". Together they made the audience want to reach out and grab hold every note. It was a night when everything came together, just like magic.*

John Coltrane

John Coltrane's rise as a musician continued as he became one of the most innovative jazz musicians of his time. In 1958, he became known for a style called "sheets of sounds," which involved playing more than one note at a time. Many of his songs had a spiritual feel, such as "A Love Supreme" and "Ascension." Coltrane died in 1967. He was honored in 1995 on a U.S. postage stamp. In 1992, he was awarded the Lifetime Achievement Award at the Grammys.

Thelonious Monk

Thelonious Monk will always be known as one of the greatest jazz musicians in history. He was featured on the front "Time Magazine" in 1964, one of only four jazz musicians ever so honored. He continued to entertain until the 1970s when he retired. Monk died in 1982. He was featured on a US postal stamp in 1965. In 1993 he was awarded the Lifetime Achievement Award at the Grammys. His song "Round Midnight" is one of the most recorded jazz standards.

THELONIOUS M

* No one knew for several decades that the concert that night at Carnegie Hall had been taped by The Voice of America Radio. The recording was discovered in 2005 at the Library of Congress by a recording lab supervisor. The recording was restored and released the same year. You can now listen to "Nutty" and "Monk's Mood" just like it sounded on that evening after Thanksgiving in 1957.

www.ingramcontent.com/pod-product-compliance
Lightning Source LLC
LaVergne TN
LVHW072125070426
835511LV00003B/92

9781630662493